# A Week of Lullabies

Compiled and Edited by
**HELEN PLOTZ**
Illustrations by
**MARISABINA RUSSO**

Greenwillow Books, New York

**D**own with the lambs,
up with the lark,
Run to bed children
before it gets dark.

*from* THE ANNOTATED
MOTHER GOOSE

To the memory of my husband, Milton,
and to all our grandchildren — H.P.

To Hannah, Sam, and Ben — M.R.

# The Week

## Monday
A Christmas Lullaby by Margaret Hillert  4
Good Night by Aileen Fisher  6

## Tuesday
Good Night by Nikki Giovanni  8
Lullaby by John R. Plotz  10

## Wednesday
When everything has drawn to a Close
   by Karla Kuskin  12
Sleep, Sleep, Sleep  adapted from the Yiddish
   by Elizabeth Shub  14

## Thursday
The Admiration of Willie by Gwendolyn Brooks  16
Sweet and Low by Alfred Lord Tennyson  18

## Friday
Early Dark by Elizabeth Coatsworth  20
Bedtime Mumble by N. M. Bodecker  22

## Saturday
Lullaby, oh lullaby! by Christina Rossetti  24
All Asleep by Charlotte Pomerantz  26

## Sunday
What Happens to the Colors? by Jack Prelutsky  28
Dear Father by Margaret Wise Brown  30

# A CHRISTMAS LULLABY

Hushaby, rockaby, softly to sleep,
Soft as the snow that is drifting and blowing.
Hushaby, rockaby, shadows are deep
Blue on the snow that is endlessly snowing.
Sleep like the animals sleepily curled
In soft little nests in a winter white world.
Hushaby, rockaby, till the stars creep
Into a day that is shining and glowing.

—MARGARET HILLERT

# GOOD NIGHT

Father puts the paper down
to say good night,
and his mustache prickles
when he hugs me tight.

Mother sets her knitting bag
beside her chair
and asks me if I've washed myself
and brushed my hair.

Grandma says, "Keep covered.
Sweet dreams to you."
And I feel quite sleepy
when "good nights" are through.

—AILEEN FISHER

# GOOD NIGHT

Goodnight Mommy
Goodnight Dad

I kiss them as I go

Goodnight Teddy
Goodnight Spot

The moonbeams call me so

I climb the stairs
Go down the hall
And walk into my room

My day of play is ending
But my night of sleep's in bloom

—NIKKI GIOVANNI

# LULLABY

Cat's in the alley
Flower's in the pot
Moon's in the sky and
Baby's in the cot

Tree and the lamppost
Standing by the door
Big dog is sleeping
On the kitchen floor

Now nighttime is falling
There are shadows all around
Baby's gonna sleep
Till the sun shines down

Mama and Papa
Are standing by your bed
Sweet dreams are coming
To fill your sleepy head

—JOHN R. PLOTZ

# Wednesday

When everything has drawn to a close.
When games are done
And friends are gone from sight
You
And the tired mice
The nesting rabbits
Go to your sleep
As I put out the light.
I'm night.

—KARLA KUSKIN

# *Wednesday*

## SLEEP, SLEEP, SLEEP

Sleep, sleep, sleep
Father's gone to town
What will he bring? A loaf of bread
God bless baby's head

Sleep, sleep, sleep
Father's gone to town
What will he bring? Two cherry pies
God bless baby's eyes

Sleep, sleep, sleep
Father's gone to town
What will he bring? A woolen vest
God bless baby's chest

Sleep, sleep, sleep
Father's gone to town
What will he bring? Three silver charms
God bless baby's arms

Sleep, sleep, sleep
Father's gone to town
What will he bring? A special treat
God bless baby's feet

Sleep, sleep, sleep

—A YIDDISH FOLK SONG, ADAPTED BY ELIZABETH SHUB

*Thursday*

# THE ADMIRATION OF WILLIE

Grown folks are wise
About tying ties
And baking cakes
And chasing aches,
Building walls
And finding balls
And making planes
And cars and trains—
And kissing children into bed
After their prayers are said.

—GWENDOLYN BROOKS

# Thursday

## SWEET AND LOW

Sweet and low, sweet and low,
    Wind of the western sea,
Low, low, breathe and blow
    Wind of the western sea!
Over the rolling waters go,
Come from the dying moon and blow,
    Blow him again to me;
While my little one, while my pretty one, sleeps.

Sleep and rest, sleep and rest,
    Father will come to thee soon;
Rest, rest, on mother's breast,
    Father will come to thee soon;
Father will come to his babe in the nest,
Silver sails all out of the west
    Under the silver moon
Sleep, my little one, sleep, my pretty one, sleep.

—ALFRED LORD TENNYSON

*Friday*

## EARLY DARK

Night's all right
With stars and a moon,
But night's all wrong
In the afternoon!
It drops from the trees
And it creeps on the floor,
And they call me in
By half past four!

—ELIZABETH COATSWORTH

# BEDTIME MUMBLE

A cherry pip,
a turnip tip,
a snippet in the snow,
a snail, a rail,
a lobster tail,
the guppy has no toe.

A honeybee,
a money tree,
a day without a sorrow,
a dime, they say,
is here today
and gone again tomorrow.

A summer song,
a winter long,
a mumble for your yawning,
"Good-by, good-by!"
the day-birds cry,
"and see you in the morning."

—N. M. BODECKER

# Saturday

Lullaby, oh lullaby!
Flowers are closed and lambs are sleeping,
    Lullaby, oh lullaby!
Stars are up, the moon is peeping;
    Lullaby, oh lullaby!
While the birds are silence keeping,
    (Lullaby, oh lullaby!)
Sleep, my baby, fall a-sleeping,
    Lullaby, oh lullaby!

—CHRISTINA ROSSETTI

*Saturday*

# ALL ASLEEP

A lamb has a lambkin,
A duck has a duckling,
And I have a baby,
Good night,
Good night,
I have a baby,
Good night.

An owl has an owlet,
A pig has a suckling,
And I have a baby,
Good night,
Sleep tight,
I have a baby,
Good night.

Even a frog
Has a wee polliwog,
And I have a baby.
Star light,
Star bright,
I have a baby.
Good night.

—CHARLOTTE POMERANTZ

*Sunday*

# What Happens to the Colors?

What happens to the colors
when night replaces day?
What turns the wrens to ravens,
the trees to shades of gray?

Who paints away the garden
when the sky's a sea of ink?
Who robs the sleeping flowers
of their purple and their pink?

What makes the midnight clover
quiver black upon the lawn?
What happens to the colors?
What brings them back at dawn?

—Jack Prelutsky

# *Sunday*

Dear Father,
hear and bless
Thy beasts and
singing birds,
And guard with
tenderness
Small things
that have
no words.

—MARGARET WISE BROWN

# TIME TO RISE

A birdie with a yellow bill
Hopped upon the window sill,
Cocked his shining eye and said:
"Ain't you 'shamed, you sleepy-head?"

—ROBERT LOUIS STEVENSON

## ACKNOWLEDGMENTS

*Permission to reprint copyrighted poems
is gratefully acknowledged to the following:*

Atheneum Publishers, Inc., for "Bedtime Mumble" from *Snowman Sniffles and Other Verse* by N. M. Bodecker. Copyright © 1983 by N. M. Bodecker.

Bramhall House, a division of Clarkson N. Potter, Inc., for "Down with the Lambs" from *The Annotated Mother Goose,* Introduction and Notes by William S. and Ceil Baring-Gould. Copyright © 1962 by William S. and Ceil Baring-Gould.

Greenwillow Books (A division of William Morrow & Company), for "All Asleep—I" from *All Asleep* by Charlotte Pomerantz. Copyright © 1984 by Charlotte Pomerantz; and "What Happens to the Colors?" from *My Parents Think I'm Sleeping* by Jack Prelutsky. Copyright © 1985 by Jack Prelutsky.

Grosset & Dunlap, Inc., for "Early Dark" from *The Sparrow Bush* by Elizabeth Coatsworth. Copyright © 1966 by Grosset & Dunlap, Inc.

Harper & Row Publishers, Inc., for "The Admiration of Willie" from *Bronzeville Boys and Girls* by Gwendolyn Brooks. Copyright © 1956 by Gwendolyn Brooks Blakely; "Dear Father" from *A Child's Good Night Book* by Margaret Wise Brown (Addison Wesley). Copyright © 1943, 1950 by Margaret Wise Brown; "Good Night" from *Out in the Dark and Daylight* by Aileen Fisher. Copyright © 1980 by Aileen Fisher; and Poem #29 "When everything has drawn to a close" from *Any Me I Want to Be* by Karla Kuskin. Copyright © 1972 by Karla Kuskin.

Margaret Hillert, for "A Christmas Lullaby." Copyright © 1969 by Margaret Hillert.

John R. Plotz, for "Lullaby."

Elizabeth Shub, for "Sleep, Sleep, Sleep," a Yiddish folk song. Translation and adaptation copyright © 1988 by Elizabeth Shub.

William Morrow & Company, for "Good Night" from *Vacation Time* by Nikki Giovanni. Copyright © 1980 by Nikki Giovanni.

Gouache paints were used for the full-color art. The typeface is ITC Leawood.

Collection copyright © 1988 by Helen Plotz
Illustrations copyright © 1988 by Marisabina Russo Stark

Books, a division of William Morrow & Company, Inc., 105 Madison Avenue, New York, N.Y. 10016.

Printed in Hong Kong by South China Printing Co.
First Edition

10 9 8 7 6 5 4 3 2 1

Library of Congress Cataloging-in-Publication Data

A Week of lullabies.
Summary: An illustrated collection of lullabies and bedtime poems by authors including Nikki Giovanni, Tennyson, and Jack Prelutsky, grouped by days of the week.

1. Sleep—Juvenile poetry. 2. Lullabies. 3. Children's poetry. [1. Bedtime—Poetry. 2. Sleep—Poetry. 3. Lullabies. 4. Poetry—Collections] I. Plotz, Helen. II. Russo, Marisabina, ill. PN6110.S55W44  1988 811'.008'09282  86-18458 ISBN 0-688-06652-6 ISBN 0-688-06653-4 (lib. bdg.)